NEW POEMS

➔≫

New Poems

JOHN HOLLOWAY

Charles Scribner's Sons
New York

CONTENTS

PART II

PART III

NEW POEMS

YES AND NO

My greedy son, once fed, withdraws
His interest and, his six teeth
Tight together, firms his jaws
Quiet as a wall: I see, beneath
That rosy skin, the son I'd choose:
To squawl and swagger and protest
Being no right man's way to refuse.
Compared—why, mere blank wall is best.

Those praters who are all excess
Or all defect, and know no speech
But colic *No* and costive *Yes*,
Might learn about what he could teach:
A trifle termed Reality,
Made up of spoons and walls and such;
Not mainly what men say and see,
But best known in the sense of touch.

Well, as he grows, let that ensure
He comes to do the same with words;
Not blustering, but serene, secure:
Walls made of flowers, walls made of birds;
Yet those same airy walls conceal
Such fluent strength as words alone
Make real; though atoms too congeal
Through motion, into quiet stone.

POOL PLACE

Never since the rockpool first
Locked its radiant dwarf sea
Where the primal tide reversed,
Showed it more tranquillity
Than we see now in these weeds
Poised in light as day recedes.

Megachronological
Spreads the deeper image, yet
Also it could be some small
Child's delight, prone on the wet
Lips to trace the sea-wrack curled
Frond by frond; or brittle knurled

Urchins and the oyster's rasped
Pachyderm. But boy's or girl's
Heedlessness would not have grasped
How the inside shell is pearls:
Nacreous light in total black,
Is that aphrodisiac

Just like bare skin to ourselves
As we unenclose its hints?
But among the rock-pool-shelves
Bivalve must conceal the tints
Lighting its inside with day;
Else the starfish tense and prey

Till that rainbow darkness tires.
All is text and paradigm:
Weedfrond round internal fires,
And we see quite plain that time
Works as usual, what is more,
Down the rock-pool-studded shore.

As we ponder, time has passed,
Darkness has begun to fall.
Luminousness does not last.

These incoming breakers sprawl
Strong and fleet as seagull's wing
Over our resistless ring

Till we find a hint of farce
Mar the image of the pool.
Things that slight perspective glass
Poises just delight the fool
In the end. So comes my wish:—
Opt for open sea, my fish.

DIAMOND

Whiteness blazed with rose and gold
Flares so cool, it cannot scorch
Even finger-tips that hold
Diamond where some hidden torch
Burns and smoulders up such lights
Through the silvers' and the whites'
Colder brightness, as must spark
Right from deep essential dark.

Kindling sharply through the whole,
What but carbon makes a jewel?
What makes carbon though, but coal?
Source of that archaic fuel
All the once gigantic ferns
Cramped to blackness: now it burns
On a fire, on a queen.
What is diamond then but green?

If our cooler qualities,
Clear, fastidious, detached,
Are what mainly warm and please
Each with each and make us matched
Crystal-wise, and largely white,
Yet let none misjudge that light:
No, let great fern-forest show
Plain, what dark it is we know

Lucidly . . . because, when deep
In the ocean of their gem
Lovers tire and fall asleep,
Mere dark is too dark for them.
Silver rather, and stone-grey
Watered light insinuates day:
Intimations where they see
Dark is one with clarity.

GALE WARNING

Cornered in the big house, all night all
Four in one room on the
Lee side thinking to windward at
The gale of the decade and
Our dead pine . . .

Two days later it was
We found the ruins of the Blenheim
Soughed in a black cascade,
Spitted, stabbed in the sod.

Fruit-loaded tree, that rendered
Me once so richly, why as I lop
Do you fight like a trapped cat?
Gnarly twigs lash, every bough
Slash up back from the ground, every stump
Jag, jab at my shin. Why as I saw
The most golden of summer's branches, I have to watch
For the torque in its fall?—the ton butt
Poising to slug my neck like a rabbit.
Cutter, do not whistle or think about a book, be
Wary to the last snick.

No wind, deep frost, thick mist.
Keep away from the pile-ups:
Take the slow road tonight, edge
To the green apple-log burning.
When from your glass and book, you hear
The wind fondling the woods, remember
Four times the height of a Blenheim,
The pine-tree's finger.

Also those houseless
On whom the sky rains
Not wood but oil and fire: a decade
Returns the jungle.

IN BINARY CODE

Passing where Thorkell the Dane in a clean
Breakthrough south had fired the woods,
I saw where the meadows greenly brushed
At the monumental cattle, and elms
Swagged and draped at the empty panes
Of the farm by the bridge.
                              I forced
The latch, stared at the void rooms
And uneven flagged floors that spoke
Of near earth. Here was a timeless
Corner of time. On the worn stairs
Had someone been scrubbing at stains, grey now
With long ago?
                    Wading the dewy
Grass to the gate, meeting the faraway
Roadman's loneliness calling after me
That farm's just gone with the woods
Sold to a man in steel, it was here
That jockey had stabbed that widow, yes,
It was good land, they wanted to spray
That weed. . . .
                    In Kazak land
Places like these are fixes, stored
By brothers of mine, in binary code.

TURNING THE TABLES

So much is the table scoured,
Now the grain is ridged with rubbing;
You could say the deal boards flowered
Into cleanliness with scrubbing;
Scrubbing makes that plain wood bright,
Lines of russet, lines of white.

Flowers and sunlight at the door
Bring a warmth to meet and wed
Coolness from the cool flagged floor.
On the table, meat and bread.
Stone and flower, beast and tree
Make the table's gaiety.

Where a loaded table glows
(Jug and tankard, plate and platter)
Round the meal there runs and flows
Gaiety of people's chatter;
As some small bird darts and twitters
So the talk here shines, here glitters.

Other rooms, another table,
All is steel, formica, glass,
Yet those people too are able
There to live as live as grass,
Sweet as timber, staunch as stone
Through humanity alone.

RAIN-GIANTS

Five days of rain along this little valley
Have muffled it in miles of hedge-high cloud to market.
A jungle of fragrances webbing at the wet house,
And the garden branded into green that hurts the eye.
The children have given names to the biggest trees:
Dark Arthur the yew, William the beech,
Dead Peter the pine . . . they pine and sigh
All night in the drift of the wind, branch their streaming
Arms as if to touch and graze at the gables.

The sheeted people turn as they sink in sleep
As quiet as ghosts . . . and then . . . sometimes, I know,
From over the skyline beyond the ruined mill
And the flares of the distant runway, and the bare down,
Far bigger creatures come more quietly still
In the empty hours. Ponderous with the past,
Deeper shades in the trees, they loiter inviting
And receding at the grey pane. Come, they say,
The way back is the way down. Come,
Through the un-mapped forest's un-taken branchways
Where the witches sing in the trees . . . They paw at the walls
Hill–high in the hills of rain, soft as clouds.

Their prints like flower–beds darkened across the grass
Are quite gone by the morning . . . I do not know
Where the rain–giants hide by day, but I know the way
Down is the way back: perhaps they lie
In the marrow of the bone until the next night.
. . . But you (at the wheel of my thought) you cannot surmise,
You of all people, what spell like a drench of gold
Sunning those giants, can float them off up the hill
Sighing like the wind?—William, Peter, Arthur
Left woodenly, airily alone?—I am filled with surprise.

PRIMARY SOURCES

I in the quiet and oak
Cores of the house stripping by
(To rest my eyes' over–reading)
The mellow of a candle. My bed
Expectant, comprehending.

                       I glimpse
From the glint of the wood, the grease
Droplets' waxy halo.

                   Along the warm
Dusk of the stubble, sheep
In Suffolk with a wool-wax grey. They stand
As still as candle-drops in the soft sun,
The mellow of October;
                  patient and
Doomed in a world of
Neon, nylon.
            I who
Nurture an ancient house, blur my
Fingers' ends to its needs, also . . .
                in a world of . . .
Until morning
And the comb–and–wattle sun
Wyandot the wall. The wind at work with
The maple beacons that flame, that flash at the
    pane.
            October argosied.
            Our nearness to a star.

Then sap of morning
At my core declares my
Primacy also. Men
Are among the burners. Reality
Their halo, they stand
Alight and seasonless. The house,
As I tend it, burnishes.

BEEF–APPLE

The ghost of a fruit-tree !
So old, yet now such a
Snow—such an icy glitter.
An ocean plant :
The boughs are flocked with flowers as
Large as sea-gulls, they
Alight, on the grey wood,
And quiver in the western wind.   A tree
Unhurriedly demanding : it
Waits, to cup its darkness, to round it
All in the red of the beef–apple.

Beef-apple !   A name in the journeyman
Sexton's country language. It fluttered from his gruff tongue
As candid as the petals.   He scattered it on the path.
Echoing, darkening :
Amber in the pebbles.

A rooted man.   Spoke like a season. Eyes sea–blue.
But wanted his way.   In the end I
Found someone else to
Odd-job my flowers into autumn.

I set my ear to the shell : all those who
Have spread their unhurried
Demanding, gull-white
Apple-wise signals I
Did not heed till they
Fell like a petal,
Those ghosts, they also
Darken this place.

CROSS–FIRE AT STRAW-BURN

Land Firers.
        I do not mean
The dogwood's watery ruby, the beacon of the
    beech the—
But the Men of autumn. They head for the fall
At war. Flaming. Invading.
The year burns.
Earth-arson, tree-arson, as
The wind quickens their fireshroud
Into sail and red shrivel. The dark
Aftermath like that shroud
On the father carried out on a door from
A six-year-old straw-blonde daughter stiff with
Bewilderment.
Staring as we did. But we, from our vehicles,
Stared sheepishly. So I now must
(Recalling it) seeing my own blonde daughter
Or if I imagine a man
To walk in circles all morning in an open field
To hide the grief his face dis–
Torted.
      Years and their winter might
Fire, erode,
——Twist, that, in its turn into
Peace, harvest.

GRAIN TO THE DAILY

A wolf in the field, look! . . . quick,
silver as a birch . . . but
of course it's a dog and
a trick of the morning light.
Yet I commend every trace,
trice of emergence
of freak and unlooked-for that riddles
regularity's doldrum: salute
that innermost ring of my friends the
mutators. They spread with
a word or a gesture their selfness,
and grey flashes silver.
Let gravitas-mongers disperse but
rarer by far is to find
in stubble a harvest again so
commend more than those,
the one who is grain to the daily:
yourself in the usual.

WINDWARD IN TWILIGHT

With the ploughland-wold alight a
light for distance, a winter
pallid sharpness, acid enough
(being edged by the
wind) to eat away clouds and
eat away me—expose where I
keep my lucid my
radiant recallings: friends
of a wintry and radiant
distinction. . . but this you
would coolly accept even
take with a hinted warmth such as grows
within like a seed as I . . .
with the ploughland-wold alight . . .
climb windward in twilight to
post you this letter.

SPEECH IN A TRAIN OR BAR BUT

For the great bird-flock—a black
crop through the stubble, in
its rising the air grew
heavy with feathers, they
reared like a wold—
I and the stranger both
had stopped and stared.
                      and we waved
as we went in casual
token of kinship that
men good–will, over the world,
freely as birds: free
speech in a train or bar.
                    but
that flock the darkened air
swirled transformingly and
itself sang with, touched
another touch also: sense
of dropping into valleys, shadows
cloud–ample, a rich
darkness of togetherness.
                   friends
share it a little but
in some I see it
born, it engendered.

PLANTING

Gently, willingly, the earth's dark opening
Embeds my spade.   A luscious tilth, rich
As molasses.   It lies, open house, for the root.

I think of seeing, among these, that take
The wind from my hand, as I straighten up, others
Of another standard, planted: think to see
The cowards of the kingdom.   Two words their tongue runs
    wanting:
No, also Yes.   They hum, haw, and then
Crumple.   Tall stacks, blown by the wrecker.
What their fine-cut tweeds drape is, limbs
Yard-armed out by a window-dresser.   Men
Empty as mobiles.
                Let me have them here,
With their arms all branching.   Grounded up to the girdle,
Hock, haunch—deep in the loam, is how I'd tread them.
Mulch them merrily.   Trust me, I'd dung them deeply.
Loosen the soil, rogue the land of weeds,
Lop, top and root-prune.   Planted among the maidens,
That draw like a smoke on the soil all spring, let them
Be re-grown over years.
             The earth is big, a man
With a spade, small.   I obscure at the work, turning
The soil and my great deeds over.   Maybe my sons
Will tell their women, as they drowse and darn,
Of the Fabian general.   Granitic, giant withdrawals
That end in the loam at the bottom of an old orchard,
Yard-armed and sweating.

            Darkly the spit turns.
The orchard is nearly full.   With a stately tread,
Stalking like the Ghost in Hamlet down and down,
I assume my rights like a skirt, gather and pull
At the black weave.   Neighbour, heel me in.
Now to be a tree.

OF THE PLAIN WAY

I believe the farmers hate
My flower-laden paddock. Three years I
    Wrenched at the hay with the rotary
Roaring, stinking, stalling on the hummocks:
    Now, I have learnt such wisdom
As whispers along the black scythe-blade's
    Silver brim: work
Only to the sound of kisses. Dry
    To the crisp stalk, to the green
Leaf of the grass, the river opens
    His mouth, takes in a flood
As arm, loin, grow to the cut,
    As scythe and row swing,
Swath, of their own: weight and counterweight
    To a man who turns to a clock.
The black bob ticks. Cant
    The cut to a tussock: the iron
Grows deft as a penknife: When it begins
    To jag at the hay, the oiled
Hone, let it scythe the scythe, at the just
    Judged angle again.
But timekeeper, watch your streaming dark
    That flows in a whistle, or
You drown in your own stain on the grass:
    Wariness, also, makes
Sinew, nerve of the plain way.

FLAGSTONES

'Hooray and up she . . . !'
'Just as the sun was rising . . .'
—A gaiety breaks through the house, over
The broad of the flagstones—humped
With time and the footstep; now
They are grey . . .
                  the brush to them!
Soap, the brimming bucket.   The elbow
Burns, and the dirt
Swishes in a suddy tide the sunshine breaks on
So that light floats up from the floor; an
Emergence of rose
And of gold, fruit–hues, warmth from the cold
Stone, from the daily grey . . .
                    as the dew warms,
The earth rubs the sun with its mountains;
A glimmer from the hillside orchard
Brushes at the mist . . .
                morning tinges; the ghost–like
Lovers, their blood mounts at
Return of the prodigal light; flush, blush and
Resume their giving and—
    'Blow away the morning dew . . .'
Bannered and felicitous, labour
Unlaboured, a gift a
Habit of humans or the ground, light as
In the flower unbreaking: so
With the arm, let it
Clean or be making as lightly as sun–up
Or the song of a man
Who sings as he scrubs.

RIVER MOVEMENT

From the word-bath of every day I
    Return in silence.
I climb, then coast down the windy ridge
    My house is earthed on.
The Glem and the short Kennet taper
    Their head—water—fingers
Toward my coming: a woman who seems
    To poise a gift.
Emptily all profuse summer,
    But winter rings
Her hands with a cold bell music. From village
    To village the dark
Penned cattle wade and munch
    The cream of their fodder;
And nostril in transient spouts: silver
    Proximate music
Breathed as they mingle for warmth. Also,
    Dis-embodied
In darkness, the mating owls waver,
    Quaver in a croon.
Difficult not to suppose that love
    Runs also here
Somehow, through the melody of creatures. Easier
    Heard if you like than
When summer tirades from the stems, radiantly
    Wayfaring, weighting
Every hedge, and the Glem and Kennet
    Fall into silence
And follow—pondered, gradual—the moving
    Of equinoxes.
Rivers, you taper your hush and mingle
    Into a knower.
I who received, into my quickness
    Such a slowness
As, summer or water—fingering winter,
    Ran like a river;
I who was gifted, profused, discern all
    People as music
Earthed and wordless, a weighting with silence a
    Woman with a gift.

REFLECTIONS AT THE FORGE

The blacksmith gruffed at me
To look at his hammer-haft. When I took
Its rise and hollow, shapely as a limb,
Burnished down to the grain, a worked wood
Married to the horny thumb, I could

Not but see the mate of
Such a rosy dermis as (layer of
Horn, layer of light, granular
Bed, make skin) you spread—lotus on dark
Lake when the first birds

Flash the day with a tune like
Horny-ended fingers of the fiddler
Hammer, a trill that fills the room
With an ample, an iron ringing: richness of air
Like petal or silent woman at—

But a child's eyes are sharp:
'When the sparks go starry,' she says, 'He'll
Begin playing his tune: pick me
Up quick' . . . The iron rings a wheel of sparks
Hissed in a red spurt

Spoked from the anvil. A flower
Flushed from the beak, it rings its (light
As crystal or a gay quaver) morning
Birdsong around, inside, everywhere over that
Glowing and rosy cooling.

MEETING POINT

Squalltalk and mizzle-talk.
We dissolve in a weather of words: remaining, our
    Parchment and deadwood. Talkative
    Weather of the window writes
        More musical music,

    And its cool descant duets
In with the buds. The wind-touched plants
    In a metronome quiet are proud
    From the humus. Tree-sap at work,
        Wines of spring like

    Claret stored in the haw and
A wet-fresh, brown maturing, crisp
    In the hazel: self–divulged
    At the mute instant of winter.
        The tree, served,

    Prepares the big turn–over
Of spring in a wordless economy. Planted
    Humbleness toiling at easy
    Achievement for men the major,
        The creative epoch

    Also. And you, as I write
Or listen, enlarge in my mind; and I think of
    That year's-pleasant-thing we also
    Rooted, perfected in silence,
        Let flower.

FROST SCHERZO.

Landscape affluent with jewel
From a simple loss of heat
From this tilted planet's twist
Starward out from solar fuel,
Puff up silver at her feet!
Hang in diamond at her wrist!

Precious, maybe—yet that seems
Almost the best mode of sense
In a realm where sense is King
Log, King Stork and all; and dreams,
Dreams, comprise the object whence
Men must draw the real real thing.

Dreams the exact result of choice
For the jumble of the time,
And the chaos in our land,
They have my considered voice:
Well, hang precious then, bright rime,
At her precious foot, or hand!

A CHARM FOR THE SCORN

Demur, no but
What we untaught ourselves—
Deride
Is what we must learn: deride,
Nothing short of it, who say
'Poor old poison' as they
Step over the bodies, their
Pity not pity but a hot
Foul breath in the face.

It is
Wood that is aseptic, so I seek a
Clear sweep of the grain, resume in my ageing
The skills of the joiner, his
Chisel, plane, rasp, all things bladed and
Abrasive, to some baulk I
Cling woodenly in a sea of
The sucreous.

But do not gain by it: these edges
Point also backward. Nor can one
Take knife–edge to water.
So halt lost at a
Darkened place. Ancient woodland
The winds have tossed and crashed,
Sinking, splintering, a
Sea-like landscape; all too easy to
Fall by rising, this formless
Anger not what I sought.

So, confronting the saccharine, choose
Brininess. A chill, a tart
Tang from the west, and my wood
Scrubbed like jetsam.

              — 'Shell over
Back : . . shell
Over, back' I heard a child
Sing at the Mayo breakers. Give me a
Wave or child action, the hard
Softness of a breaker, brush the
Poison-fanciers aside, poor
Cuttlefish fragments as light as
The sea-breeze tossing them.

IN PRAISE OF FOLLY

Small foolishness, starting dandelion-wise
Our tidied-up lawns; and, yes, egg- or sun-like
Punctuating dailiness, dwarfed by its giant,
More precious and sister form, no flower but
A crop and terrain changer—or as if
Summer's clouds could shadow the ground but
Luminously—
                every day as I drive
From a corn to a stock shire I think about
Folly, and the laughter for it, ringing
In the valleys like Treble-Bob-Majors
Or birdsong or thunder or mooing. And indeed must be
(I think how folly is abounding)
Leisured or ample or ruminant.
                      A better Ulysses
Is what I would make, with all the suitors,
If any should be gorging at all,
To dance at a gay recessional. In the rain
I saw at the roadside a roadman in his up-ended
Barrow, reading a paper, laughing himself
Red at the French Head of State:
And I bless the beauty of Folly.
                         Also,
Dear and arable one, jubilant over
The big yield of it in me, remember
   —Like a giant hoopoe landing, a sunset of wings—
Your corn and land-wide kind. Lightness
That helps with the heavy of the harvest, what we enjoy
Like honey on the tongue, but sharp: reciprocity.

II

OLD SHORT WORD

It struck two o'clock, her eyes met mine, fire from a gun.
'I'm sorry,' she said; 'it's a case of the old short word.'
The weather was preparing to change. 'Is it,' I asked,
'A case of the old short word, old short word,
To lie like a hack-horse-coper, a twopenny bawd,
On the back– and the fore–hand, as easy as swill from a glass?'
'Yes, it is,' she answered. 'Is it,' I asked
(And the blue sky went green as pistachio nuts)
'A case of the word, to game it all forward and back,
On the fro, on the to, like a boy with a fish, cat
Wih a cradle?' (The green sky went purple as a plum.)
'Yes, it is,' she answered. Next I asked
'Is it a case, to be never yourself, no more
(The sky going brown as a bun) than light in a prism
That tangles its angles as you dangle the glass?'
    'Yes,
'That too,' she answered. 'Is it,' I asked her next
'A case, a case, for the mouth of a woman to taste
Aloes and sloe for the places it goes and will go?'
'Yes,' she answered, the sky blushing burgundy red,
The words I spoke being these, '———and your tongue to strike
Abrupt as the copper–head? Look! Try counting them now,
Weals from a tongue that plies at the old short word.'
The sky was flaming genteelly, like a charcoal grill
In a soft lights restaurant. 'O yes,' was what she answered,
'That's the word, that's the Real Presence of the Word.'
The sky in this country being grey, we hearing the clock
Lash two at the bell, fire from a gun.

JOHN

John the Needle-Eye Man. By the rosewood
    Shake my hand. You are cold! Let me
Offer you something superior. Port
    Robust from the bins. John the Wine–Cooler
Subdues the weather inside the earth.
    There. By the candles, I see our faces
Take shape, blandly, in the crystal. Which
    Of my mistresses ought I to loan you? The black,
Or brown, or yellow, or a pink one of course.
    Their health, and yours, And mine. You have little
To say. But John has enough. A blade
    Cascades, alight, watering. John the
Knife-Blader, Edge-Trimmer, Close-Shaver, Rat-Racer,
    Card-Sharper, Sharp-Shooter . . .
                       Why, Stranger,
Do you hump your guns on the bench? The Word–
    Spinner smooths the air with his tongue. Wind
And moon have fallen from sky. It is cold
    On the hill-side. Yes, I will pass you my coat.
John the Rag–Man. Now you hunger for
    A drink. It is red. Homer's trench
Between us, Dead Man. John Blood–Donor
    Rages like the poisoned rat. Kick him in the pit.

DOG FOX

Look. The old dog fox. Now, he knows
Three-sided rivers that bring tears to hounds'
Landseer eyes. He can make it rain. You'll not nose
Him, when he's out on his morning rounds:
These days, his brush can smell just like a rose,

And he simply squats and grins when he hears the hunt,
Because now he can turn into a hiker in tweeds,
Or the RSPCA man. His latest stunt
Is to up one pad and be a sign-post: it reads
'To The Kennels'. He watches the dogs trail off in front

Dog tired. In the season when the hares box
Among the buttercups, and bees go honeying tight
Down inside the roses, that old fox
Finds his whole body grained through with warm light;
He doesn't have to think about barnyard cocks,

He eats spring. If only he can shun the green shaws
Of one serpentine valley, and not go back
Where once a young fox thought even the flowers were hounds' jaws,
And an old fox's cunning's sure to melt before the pack . . .
But what direction keeps twitching in his paws?

MORE

William Blake by watery shore—
Some conundrum.   I don't know.
Not those Cliffs at Elsinore
Where the bloodred breakers flow.
    Early shore or mountain lark
    Once lit up the air half-darkened.
    Now it's just dogs bark, dogs bark.
What do dogs bark?   More More More.

'What a Piece of Work is Man!'
Cried the Prince.   He'll get a shock.
Who still thinks a clock-face can
Only tick out tock-tick-tock?
    No no no, give things their dues,
    Clocks are kept to keep things moving,
    Where, you ask?   The latest news
Is, for Move, read More.   More More.

Did you know that Mr. Blake
As a nude photographer
(Human form divine!) would make
After tax, five hundred per
    Cent per annum?   What, not bad?
    When the Father breathed in Adam
    Was the first word Adam said
'Blessed' . . . ?   No no no.   More More.

In the dark the great big sails
Of the great big mills go round.
Souped–up flailers flailing flails.
Lance in rest we save the pound
    Just with charging, tough and slick;
    Simulating Señor Quixote;
    In reserve is Panza's trick—
Our arse-battlecry's More More.

Venus.   Know Her? —Star of Love.
On her dust-enveloped skin
Death is King: ice-clouds above

Build a pitch-black heat within
    Save for where those ice—clouds sheen.
    Just a curious stellar greenhouse.
    Once our mariners have been
There and back . . . More More More More.

England's Green and Pleasant Land,
With the sub-soil much in view
Where the eight-lane roads are planned
(Or will be be, when plans come through).
    See the Dragon and Prince Hal
    Hotspur up the bull-dozed valley.
    Which is Prince, which Dragon?   Well,
Which cries louder, More More More?

Once a sun—burned beggar—man
Put my ignorant much-too-much
Back across my well-washed hand
His cleanness was not to touch.
    Who was poor and who was rich?
    Gaze on this and on that picture.
    I can tell you which is which
And I ask no More More More.

BIG GAME

No paths go down to the still dirty water
of the Sea House. The polychromatic ooze
dun with lightlessness. This is where
Tot the Water Giant, Mish the Big Fish,
Brush the Weed-pad, and Mash the Blue Devil
cribbage all decade . . . as light and trite as bubbles,
Hat-Peg and Peg-Top and Top the Peg-a-Ramsey
gavotte sludgily on the cribbage-board. Tot deals
a three–two–one once Brush has thoroughly
mish-mashed the shuffle. Slowly the thumbed tricks
pinnacle. Dumb, pig-eyed, William the Silent
(the Big Whale) sounds profoundly; and sometimes
sidles into the glum party. Nobody
listens to William. Well, and how could they?
William, he doesn't care. But every time
Brainwave the Deep Sea Diver drops in
blossoming down through a bright bouquet of bubbles,
assured as a war–head, what they do is cut
his lifeline and braces, give him dummy to hold,
and the game goes on. Brainwave loses, he's not
up to such low company. Tot
grins mile–wide and gobbles him. That's what happens
if you're not flush with sea–bed money. Brush
leans over and wipes where he sat: the little pegs
hornpipe and titter on the board. The next Diver drops
like an egg for boiling. Brainwave his name as well,
to be cribbed in the cribbage. When Tot swallows,
cocking his head back, look! a new pair of legs
foreshortened in bubbles and plummeting. Mash howls
and blues the water. Mish takes a trick.
William (rolling) spouts the taper out.
They play by the wavering light of the waving weed.

DRAGON AND DRAGON-FLY

A candle-end, and two odd high-heeled shoes.
(Fetish for candlelight worship?) Near them a crate
Of half-drunk wine that must have been filched.
    I had run
The tramp's-earth to earth.

He had nailed the windows blind with a sheet.
    The stone
Lay pitted, clumsy, on the floor. The cottage was sodden
With damp and dark. Its plaster melting back
To earth.
        On the earth, a cellophane sack of rags,
And the two odd shoes.
          When I heard the unshorn beast
Drenched with rain and drink—heard his heavy
Breath and tread, hand like a root flung
At the unhinged door, then I doffed my grey
Gloves-and-topper, fluent French and all my
Knowledge and disguises, yes I dreaded I threaded
I sped to the rafters. 'I spy snake or dove
That hunts in the Dead Wood,' he cried. 'Being
A human being. You Are That,' I replied.
'Save your sayings for the tombstone–mason,' he says
Stooping: 'The pigeons here have wings of glass.'
And the bottles begin to fly. Dead Men
Soar like Elijah or rockets
                  Winged I fell
To the vintage and candle–butt. My black hands root
In the rags all night for something I do not find,
But I know it is heavy as a stone.

            Later, when morning
Twined its grey up the cold shreds of cloud,
And I shaved my sea–wrack beard, as I stood
Downing at my dove waistcoat, my glance fell
On the heels on the floor.

THE TALKING BIRDS

Heartburned with indignation, fatigue
And four days' fasting,
But long-headed as ever,
He was abashed:
Perceiving, he did not eat the ravens' leavings,
But they fed him:
For when, awkwardly, they dropped
Their hunks beside his sandal,
'Lech', they called, 'Lech',
A deep, hoarse note,
Almost voicing the guttural.

Ravens, the most long-headed of birds,
Can learn truly to use, not merely speak,
A word—or maybe two—of human tongue.
(Though being but creatures, can confuse its meaning.)
To help that man in rags, distrustful, slow
To learn, and even now amid his tears,
As humans will, cursing and waving his stick,
They had taught themselves:
'Lech', they cried back, 'Eat':
What else could he have said?

But Elijah
Watching their lucid mischievous eyes,
Big glossy shoulders, a head aslant,
That one's monkey–wrench bill,
Had spoken, with arm upraised,
The good Hebrew the Lord spake to Abraham
And also to him:
'Lech', he had said, 'Lech lecha . . .'
Get thee from hence. . . . .

DRINKS AT THE WEATHERCOCK INN

A Medley for People and also Voices

Voice of the Holystone Man

Turn again, weather-cock, on your stony steeple,
Find me the proper way to look, wast as you are able:
Northern Bear or Southern Bear, the Eagle or the Wren,
Topsydom or Turvydom, but find me an honest man.

Turn again, dickory-dock, before the hour strikes.
All the honest men are fast asleep against their wives.
Fast asleep and dreaming, but men dream all alone.
Gaudeamus igitur, till dark is done.

Turn again, goldiclock, the time has come to sing;
No good sitting up on that tower with your head under your wing;
No time to sleep again, I see the morning grey;
Soon there'll be gold in them there hills, *ta-ra-ra-boum-deay*.

Weathercock

Lock the dairy door! Lock the dairy door!

Moneybags Man

Try again, weather vane, the dairies are all gone
   From Keen and Money England, where the sun has never shone;
Each expense account farmer, he has a little gun:
   Trust in the RSPCA?—Trust in Number One.

Weathercock

Try again, try again, Moneybags Man;
Cook me my goose as fast as you can;
Toast me some white bread or toast me some brown;
Or fill me with buckshot and let me fall down.

Holystone Man

Wandering alone upon the Lonely Crowd,
And treading on my brother's death beside me,
O'er vales and hills, a notice read 'Keep Out:
'Government Land, Untouched by Human Hand',

And from that jocund company I turned and fled
(Withdrawing on the firing of a gun)
And heard that music after it was heard no more.

Weathercock

I am the Fire Bird. See my breast
Burst into flames all through the hours
Before the sun reaches the west;
All my rump, golden flowers
Wind-buffeted, or breeze-caressed.

Star of the morning that the air
Takes by the tail and spin about,
High on my tower of stone I flare
So gleefully, it seems I shout:
But that's the wind, with whom I pair.

Below, all round the bells peal
And chime, the air's as bright as glass;
Blazing and shining, watch me wheel
Into the wind, as bold as brass,
As rich as gold, as sharp as steel.

Riddle

Who killed Cock Robin?
I, said Cock Robin, with my little bobbin:
Ta-ra-ra-boum-deay.

Wandering Willie Winkie's Song

Cock-a-Doodle rode to town
With his Horn of Plenty;
Master's lost his fiddling stick
And there's your *non obstante*.

The moon doth shine as bright as day,
Poor Jack has burnt the gravy;
The wind has stolen my heart away,
And there's *experto crede*.

The North Wind blows, we shall have snows,
She called me Jack-a-Dandy;
But London Bridge has broken down
And I lost my *locus standi*.

There was a man lived in the moon,
And so *sic transit* glory;
She shall have music wherever she goes,
And there's your *a priori*.

The cock sings, Lock the Dairy Door;
She was my *alter ego;*
When all the birds begin to sing
Cock Robin sings *cum grano*.

Honeypot Man's Song

What is there, Weathercock, North if I ride?
That's where the girl lives I wanted for bride;
There's an old trot who's gone blind in one eye;
Hush-a-bye baby, baby don't cry.

Air

Terra incognita, hush-a-bye-bye,
Non est inventus, when you've only one eye.

Weathercock, if I turn Eastward, what then?
    Shall I once more see my true-love again?
There's an old madam, can feel with one hand,
    Hush-a-bye baby, you'll soon understand.

What is there, weathercock, if I turn South?
    A girl there once brought my heart into my mouth:
There's an old woman, her arms in the suds,
    Did you think that the windfalls stay fresh as the buds?

Weathercock, Weathercock, if I turn West?
    That's where the girl lives that I loved the best;
She lives in the westland, beside the blue sea,
    With her rich handsome husband and little boys three.

Prolog im Himmel

The bird upon the steeple
Sits high above the people,
        But the Flowers of the Forest
        Are all weeds today.

The wedding bells are ringing,
The boys and girls are singing,
   . . . ashes, ashes,
   Let all kneel down to pray.

Ad maiorem gloriam,
Gloriam, gloriam,
   Ad maiorem gloriam
   All fall down.

Weathercock Aria

Into the wind, turning my nose of brass
Northward, I sigh in the airy tide and see
The twin towers of Dereham where Cowper died,
And Swaffham of the Great Fire. Beyond, towers
Of iron are fishing for oil in the sea; beyond,
Ice-islands and the Short Polar Hop,
And the sea red with the whales . . .

Into the wind, turning my nose of gold
Eastward, I swish in the airy current, and behold
Bury St. Edmund's ruined monastery
Acre upon acre, and beyond the sea of green
And the Green Children of Woolpit, the dead port
Of Blytheburgh, its empty church—'fire after fire'—
'Shut the door', the sexton says, 'or the birds
Get in and fly round and round till they die of thirst.'

Into the wind, turning my nose of sun
Southward, I sail on the airy stress, and listen
To the Majors of Lavenham musically pealing
At the duty of the bells: hunting and coursing, until

The 'matchless tenor' makes Eight.
                         wool and jam
From Tiptree, and the ghosts of Constable
And Gainsborough wander like dwarfs among the pylons.
Further towards the flowering of the sun,
In sleepy Seville with its Moorish palaces
(The air thickens to honey, afternoons
Warm among cliffs of light) I glimpse a man
Take a plank to the nose of a horse.

Into the wind, turning my nose of fire
Westwards, I float on the airy flow, and observe

The Lost Causes and the Dreaming Spires,
Or where the Cement Works nestle against the Fen;
And I listen for how many times they call white black,
Or take their nearest neighbour for their back,
Or tell you soberly, botch means create,
And show you all ways home, except the straight.

If I truly were Minerva's owl
Instead of just a flat, two-sided fowl,
Or if I truly were the nightingale,
Full up with song, not brass, from nose to tail,
With feathers, not this metal, for a wing,
Then I'd fly straight down off this rocky shelf,
And find a branch there, and so sweet I'd sing,
They'd wake, and think it was the Queen herself.

Travelling Viceroy's Voice

Good morning, village blacksmith, you laboured at your forge
Till very soon We gave you the Saint Michael and Saint George.

Good morning, village gardener, so well you kept the border,
Very soon We gave you the Royal Victorian Order.

Good morning, village bicyclist, so swiftly you could pedal,
That soon We had to give you the British Empire Medal.

Here's to the Empire Medal, they've earned it to a man;
But when the glass is falling, where shall We go for tan?

Briskly pass the bottle, pass it round again;
But when the glass is broken, what shall keep out the rain?

Duet

Weathercock, weathercock, where have you been?
    Round and round, round and round. What could be seen?
Moneybags, Moneybags, I dare not say;
    Make me a hay-seed, I'll hide in the hay.

Thing in Sheet

'Still through the hawthorn blows the cold wind' . . .
With dreadful Faces throng'd and fierie Armes,
For many miles about there's scarce a bush.

Heath-Storm Auf Dem Theater,
Cock Robin on the Piccolo

The Secretary reported
  One of our oldest member's
(After years of loyal service)
  Unfortunate decease;
It was agreed to minute
  The general feeling was
Nemine contradicente
  And very deep sense of loss.
        We olde men, I drede, so fare we . .

The Chairman next proposed
  (According to the Report
Recently presented to members)—
  This view found wide support.
On further consultation
  The prospect had receded:
Much fuller co-ordination
  And a fresh approach being needed.
        The flour is goon, ther is namoor to telle . . .

With reference to this matter,
  Enquiries were proceeding,
Consenting to become,
  And able to be completed.
Several distinguished persons
  Agreeing to be co-opted,
Were fulfilling a vital need;
  But this was not adopted.
        But Lord Christ, whan that it remembreth me . .

Intimately related
  (The Treasurer drew attention)
To these considerations
  Had had to be back–dated
Unless to the effect that
  Possibilities were mooted
But no decision taken
  And the business then concluded.
        O ryng, fro which the ruby is out falle . . .

Wandering Willie Winkie

. . . a little fire in a wild field, is
man no more than this? Hog
in sloth, fox in stealth, lion in prey,
in the voice of a nightingale. Set not
thy heart on proud array,
thou art the thing itself.

This Same Learned Theban

There was a little man, and he had a gammy leg,
   And he shot his little dad really dead, dead, dead.
Then he went a little way, and he had a lucky day,
   And he tumbled his mother into bed, bed, bed.

Then there came a dread disease, till he went down on his knees,
   And the parson said the truth would come out soon, soon, soon;
When it did, he took a pin, and his eyes he stuck it in,
   Till he couldn't tell the sun from the moon, moon, moon.

Said by A Human Being

Oedipus, Odysseus and so on
Have always impressed us
As making rather a fuss.
Of course, we do have our own standards:
Ours is a rough, masculine island;
We chose it after exhaustive tests
For real quality and also public opinion.
Whatever your sex, you will find it just right.
What we offer is Crete without the Minotaur;
Or maybe just a tickle, a tingle of Minotaur
If you really want it.

But we think our new miracle sunshine—
The kind that's really
Natural
And warms actually from right inside . . .
(You're with us, we hope . . . ?)
Leaving that deep brown tan,
Either pearly, rosy, or transparent, the choice is yours
(And you may also like to know
We've eliminated sun-spots)
Together with our non-fattening food, our wine

With such a kick in it, although of course
Just right for driving round the island after dinner
At a silky-smooth, rough-masculine speed;
And our husky, dusky maidens,
Carefully selected from many distant lands
To make the island's oldest tradition . . .
Will intrigue you.

Science and the archaic way of life.
It's a real marriage.
Here you are able to completely be yourselves.
And however low you sink,
Our specially-prepared nondrowning water will take care of things.
By the way:
Visitors are kindly requested
Not to look at the rock-carvings;
Which are eternally young, and live in an older world,
But these bull-headed men, man-headed birds, and many-headed serpents

Are not part of our chosen way of life.

Holystone Man

Tired with all these, I drop my hand
Upon the scrubbing brush and soap
And sharp sweet purifying stone
That names me—and I drudge and grope
All the night through, to scrub and scour
Each tower and bell and each bell–rope.

And every space and road between:
Scouring the decks all ways I go,
I slop the water from my pail,
The untiring arm brings out the glow;
The beauty of the holystone
Being to turn you white as snow.

Soap, water, and a burning heart,
I pass from land to land all night;
The beauty of the holystone
Being to turn all darkness bright;
The beauty of the holystone
Being to leave you clean as light.

Queen of The Air

Holystone, holystone, knock at my door,
Scrub my house at a quarter to four;
A quarter to four is mid-summer dawn;
    Turn, intruder;
Turn in the darkness, reap the corn.

Weathercock–Robin's Drinking Song

Holystone Man, I have a thing to say:
That all this tale of scour and toil and scrub
Is simply so much water down the drain:
So better far think twice before you drudge.
As far as eyes can see or legs can go,
Levavi oculos, then round again,
The South brings sunshine and the North wind snow.

Maiorem gloriam, up here aloft,
Spreads everywhere as I go round and round;
You, *de profundis,* surely catch my drift,
So let the Jack go work and sit you down;
And listen to my tale, you great and small,
From where I make the tower's golden crown:
Come up, you'll find that swinging pays for all.

Or if the cards fall out, that you must drum
In a pint pot, Stone Man, just tell me this:
Why see red morning skies each evening-time?
Over the hills and far away is best,
You keep on singing; but my favourite catch
Runs simply, *meum est propositum*
To step inside and neatly snick the latch.

Sederunt: as I do here hour by hour.
Much is like much, and many comes from one.
Nosce teipsum. Perched up high, I pour
My patch of darkness down: but from the sun,
Or faintly from the moonlight as you sleep;
Then watch the cool dawn un-veil all the flowers;
Better by far look twice before you weep.

Part

III

LONDON, GREATER LONDON
(After Juvenal, Satire III)

Well, it really hurts, to think of him going away.
But he's made the right decision: that's got to be faced,
For what could be worse than—well, yes, the horrors of London
(Culminating in the Festival of Poetry)? . . . His station waggon
Was crammed the day he went. I joined him as far as Richmond,
Through the publishers moved up west, and the Royal Car Parks,
And the spacious villa Estates in the Green Belt.
This is what he said: 'It's unliveable–in:
Get's worse every day; so I'm off, before I'm senile.
Agreed, it's a real break—but what's the good?
How can I cope with London? When a book's bad,
I just can't say it was 'deeply moving' and 'I wonder
if you'd care to inscribe my copy . . . ?' I haven't read Jung.
Don't know any abortionists. Can't play bingo.
It may be the place if you want a coffee–coloured model
Or a Vietnam gymnastics–mistress: but it's not me.
Never mind if they come from Halifax, Oldham, Sydney,
The New Men, New Mannikins, if they don't know about culture
And play the guitar, well, they're so smooth, they're glass;
In those bum–freezer tuxedos, you'd think they were waiters.

And they make for London like waiters. First, they act as
The company soil–pipes; a bit later on, you find
They're all on the Board. Quick Wits, a Bloody Nerve,
All the Answers—and for numbers! It's Cup Final Day.
Smart! Is This Your Choice? He's playing it.
Linguistics, mathematical logic, advertising copy,
Action painting, judo, market forecasts, compering,
Psychiatry, cybernetics—he even knew Sabrina.
The Other–directed Man. Say Fly, he's airborne.
And the knock–out, this one's not from a Comprehensive School
Or College of Advanced Technology: First, Modern Greats, he is,
And 'a poet in his own right.' Can't I dodge their gent's suiting?
Well, we're all entertainers now. Are you laughing? He nearly died.
Pull a long face, he's doubled it (grinning arsewise).
Say it's chilly, he's buttoning his British Warm. Say it's hot.
He's Talking About Jerusalem, he's dripping. We're non–starters
And as far as Sex goes, Is Nothing Sacred?

Seems the right approach. Respectable married woman,
Teenagers, model husband, nice young man, the lot.
And if that's no good, tries it on with granny on a pension.
All to get the inside news and pull the right strings.

And since we're on the subject, just take a look at
Our educational establishments; that's where you find
The real outsize fiddles. Heads jockeying for places
At the older universities. Lethal testimonials:
'Feel it my duty to add . . .' Public lecturers
Asking for their fee in notes. One day they'll steal
The hairs out of Pegasus's tail: that'll finish it.

There's no place for an ordinary Englishman here.
They want it all, with their well–bred adverse comments
In the Director's ear, drip drop, they don't need to learn how,
They were born dripping. 'Much regret no vacancy occurs
At present,' we read. Just one more off the waiting list.
No good living in a dream–world: it won't get you anywhere,
Out of bed early to go to a Shareholders' Meeting,
Buttoning your pants as you run . . . 'That concludes our business.'
He's having lunch with an American widow or a model.
'Darling why did you stay so long at that horrid committee?'
After all, they can spend the works' monthly wage-bill on a girl,
But if some high-class piece takes your fancy, you'd think
Twice before you asked her to flash-of-white-thigh out of her Mark X
For you: what about those little red figures dancing at the bank?

Go up for an interview, take authenticated copies
Of your qualifications, and they'll make 'discreet enquiries'
About your means. That'll tell them, in case you don't know,
Whether you're a security risk. 'How big's his wages–roll?
Is he farming?' (Inland–Revenue–wise). 'How many courses
Does Mrs. Applicant serve at her little dinner parties?'
'Just a few more questions about your financial status . . .'
Which will tell us if you're ethical, you see. The poor man
(Underprivileged I mean) can swear himself blue in the face,
They're taking careful note of his expression of view.
Anything else? Yes. If he's wearing off–the–pegs,
Or his socks dangle, or you glimpse a potato–heel,
Or his collar's not trubenized, or you can see
Where his wife's been stitching at him, it's 'really rather funny.'
Poverty, poverty, what have you worse than this?—
The poor man knows he can find a grin in every smile.

'If you don't mind,' you hear, 'This is a reserved compartment.'
So it is. As you go, you see your places taken by
The sons of ponces, who first saw the light in a clip–joint,
Or a disc–jockey's offspring, a bouncer's, an all–in wrestler's,
A boxing tout's (all been to good schools of course).
Well, I suppose the Prince Consort first thought up First Class Carriages.

Have you ever heard 'a marriage has been arranged'
Into this income–bracket when the young man's not even
Paying at the Standard Rate—let alone, no portfolio
That bulges . . . the way the bride does? Do 'persons of limited means'
Ever get the jackpot legacy? Or made an Alderman?
(I mean in The City, obviously.) It's high time such people started
A New Life somewhere, maybe in Our Great Commonwealth.
The able boy has to fight his home background
The whole way . . . and life in London's worst,
The cost of living's so high. Hospitality, tips,
Even eating out by yourself is really quite something.

In some parts of the country, perhaps, folk don't ride
In a car, till the hearse knocks at the door. Even now
Have gymkhanas and village fêtes, and the children don't call
Westerns *vieille vague*. Men's clothes don't run after the fashion,
And the cops don't drive white Jags. But where we are
It's the Affluent Society to the gusset (Extended Play,
Extended Payments, Creative Fares, and everybody Conforming Upwards).
Monnet talks. The firm is happy to celebrate
Our prospective entry into E.E.C. *(Ha ha.)* All personnel
Cordially invited. Something for the kiddies. Tickets five
Guineas excluding drinks (doubles? but naturally).

You tell me who could get run over in Lundy Island,
Ardnamurchan, Wells-next-the-Sea, Durness?
But here it's all underpasses, motor-ways, twelve-mile jams, and
Articulated lorries jack-knifing downhill in the smog,
And a hundred deaths on the Road each Day of National Rejoicing.

If you could only forget What's On,
And Keeping Abreast, I know just the sort of thing
Would suit you down to the ground: think what a snip
You could pick up in Dorset, the Cotswolds, unspoilt Suffolk
(Beyond commuter country of course)—and be paying less
Or at least no more than key-money on a mews in Chelsea.
A matured garden (with all main services though),

Then take up roses for pleasure, especially old roses,
And give modest select dinners in flawless taste.
Not gracious—distinguished living. And surely it's something
Even to have one pony for your only daughter to learn on
. . . There really has been a Decline, a Falling Away—
You could put it so much better than I. Merrie England;
The organic community; a living tradition; wheelwrights.
The old fashioned kind of J.P.—and just the village stocks.
Well, I mustn't dawdle; it's getting towards rush-hour,
I'll be stuck on the by–pass . . . keep in touch . . . I'll look you up
When you're settled at Chipping Camden. Yes, that could tempt me,
It's nippy sometimes on the coast; and I've always been one for hills.'

That's what he said. I thought he put it frightfully well.

BRIEF LIVES

I—Churching

give hearty thanks
thou hast delivered

    the father
    be her tower

the sun shall not burn
going out and
coming in.

II—Baptism

come these infants
suffer
little children
give thyself to this transitory

vain flesh desires glory
give thyself to
innocency of
this transitory

life a man ought to
know and believe
his soul's health

credo

III—Confirmation

my hands picking and stealing
my tongue evil speaking
to get my own living

thou art not able
thou art bound

what dost thou chiefly learn?

rehearse.

IV—Matrimony

undefiled members

an excellent mystery
an estate in paradise
my body is a pledge
with my lusts and beasts
for better for richer
men are bound to love

let him now
the hid man which is in the heart
love and
depart

unto the third and fourth

or
hereafter for ever
hold his

peace

beati omnes

V—Visitation of the Sick

he hath laid me

I stretch forth
I am become a monster
my tongue all the day long
after this painful life
everlasting
thy accustomed sickness

it shall turn to your profit

speravi

our door into

gladly

death

VI—The Communion of the Sick

verily I say unto

all men be subject

all men in a readiness

VII—Burial

cut down the secrets of our hearts
the strangers and widows
but a short time
cast upon the body

a natural body
flesh and blood cannot inherit
we shall be changed
it shall turn into
a flower in the midst of life

dilexi

whosoever believeth in
the earth
the last enemy is
a shadow

quemadmodum
all other departed
death is thy sting

the trump shall be changed man
a quickening of the

incorruptible

earth.

SHAKESPEARE AND THE BIBLE

how goes the	night	boy?
	burn	t out and so am I
to spy her through the	wall	when madman lead
the	blind	her hook shall
be of	gold	in the dead waist
and middle of the	night	better to
marry than to	burn	now we
grope for the	wall	like
the	blind	but I have gathered
silver and	gold	be
content a naughty	night	to
swim in our throne	burn	ed the waters
were a	wall	on the right hand
and left a gift doth	blind	the eye here's
poison and here's	gold	

THE COUNTRY OF NOTHING

This being the country of nothing . . .
    Of Nothing? no, but of nothing
finished: it being simple folly
    to enquire for a finished article:
and demanding perfection itself showing
    perfection not to exist—
make it a not untoward time
    to locate a succinctness: such
as resides in a leaving something unsaid or
    simply the hint of unsaying.

Let a man be speaking, yet
    before him he sees faces
blank with a not grasping, or not
    wanting to grasp; or perhaps
something short of blank, unless
    blankness amounts to a surly
and afraid sureness. to see that,
    no need to travel far:
but to see a face blank with a kind
    of kind quiet—a knowing
it barely matters not to grasp,
    to leave unassailed, unsaid,
it will come right over time, a man
    need go no further, maybe,
than his pillow.
              Somewhere, maybe,
    (in a garden or sight of the sea)
the child listens to the man. her face
    alight with a heedfulness
that grows into growing. now she takes
    her fingers and paper, her bowed
head labours her hand at the page.
    half, the giant who lives
in the wood on the way to school, and his wife
    in the pines, are a joke; and here
the other half towers and stalks
    in a crayon storm . . . let
a man be speaking of things his hand
    subdued to a script and years

can never sketch again, the child
       who listens alight takes
a word for her stormy image, if
       —no but only if—he can fall
silent at the half–said thing; half
       a grasping and half the sheer
making flash that comes in a growing:
       but the child being father to the man,
it is always a matter of the half: to re–make in
       the wise quiet of the speaker,
wise in quiet and plainness. therefore
       (to aim, again, at the brief)
deal, please, the next hand
       of images face down:
the usual and also the seemly way,
       and a man has nothing to add.

the making light that is always a growing:
       and thus, a poet (to give
a new toot on the old horn)
       and as much, a woman's hands
that dredge the dry flour, and change
       their kneading at the need of a cake;
and thus the planter stancing the sapling
       for its boughs to bow with the wind;
and thus a man, breaking off
       in the middle of what he says;
hearing his own muddled word
       hurry, wrong, from his lips.
apprehension.   one knows the wide
       open eye that sees
nothing more, than a pane of glass
       that glares from an empty house.

consult for the right way: the right
       avert their gaze from nits
straining for lousehood: gently, the right are
       unprepared to see
busy-bodies, as really the same as
       the pelican in her piety:
and need no lens, in order to
       discriminate those who cherish

a single fixed and firm and unquenchable
       intent: that goes by the name of
advantage.   here, let all men
       recall, the high ape
it is, most shows his tail.
       nor does one need to screw
one's eyes up to spy those who cry
       'all's well!' . . . right up to
the bang.   neither warrants extensive
       review; nor any more than
such movement of a man's shoulder
       as is both a shrug and a bracing.
and should it be, that men decline
       to give heed, except to
excess, thank you, one elects
       the pose of a post: a little
wooden, but having a certain clear if
       limited merit: to be upright.
since (always without embitterment)
       all such things as those a
man may go so far as to have in
       derision.   lay it to heart . . .
for there is the clear knowledge: make
       transparent . . . to which end
let all opt for the optical: simply, the
       lens; through the glassy
nothing of which, emerges a focus.
       the rule of the lens, brought
softly, out of opacity into
       translucency, then the trans—
parent, by time, merely; and abrasion.
       there is much to be said for abrasion.

—but besides this, there exists a way of
       laughing in kindness that ought
to be seen as a welcome.   here a man can
       know his follies are known
without scorn: gentleness knows,
       gentleness briefly knows.   yet
hidden in gentleness lies a secret
       known, one infers, to few:

yet the few who possess that secret
	know their brevity for the
source and mate and mother and twin of
	joy. yes, of joy.
the whole of life at a point; and there,
	there is nothing to see; nor,
listening, to hear; because, it makes
	nothing of something; blood
like air, and air itself a rich
	giver. therein lies
the standing of a man: simply, a man
	transformed to a sun; arising,
raised, exulting, exalted—out of
	the status of the creatures, and a woman who
also, bowing her head at a sink or
	laundering, thinks she has been a
giver or a taker in this, let her—
	let her stand re–assured.

the country of joy.   achieved and serene,
	it records its achievement; the settled
feature of a middle voice.   and now
	that it stands created, and all
finished and intact, discredits all
	excess; posture; and also
itself.   this being the country
	of echo without the echoed; and
no one is grounded in safety because
	the mould itself is electric, is
dark with its smouldering danger.   here
	the great lights fork and
flash from a blue sky; great
	thunder lacks the admonitory
flash first: long drought
	is what spates the becks; it is June
suns hang rime on the full-blown blossom; the
	open meadows are full
of invisible ambushes, darkness sparkles with
	black flames but scorching
needle-points hang in the morning breeze
	light as motes of dust and
—and most, it is I, it is I, it is I!

I think not.   for if it
is true, this daylight is such a dazing as
        is a version of darkness—that
is other than for thunder and lightning; other
        than the greedy scream of the self.
a dark opalescence from strangeness.   consider
        the luminous night of the flower's
innermost throat (without changing
        its opulence) magnified into
a whole country: about it flies
        the silver dove and golden
crow made by ordinary morning
        sun, that lights also
even the wind, inter-leaving
        the leaves with gold: enhancing
and making light of summer; and rain's
        laundering washes a green
light, up, out of the leaves, to be
        the making flash of summer
finished and simple, that is always a growing
        into the brief, enormous
miracle of the daily; dark country
        of a light nothing.   see!
it opens in a view of the sea.   the line
        that bounds it just a succinctness
and edge, something unsaid, open–
        ended, unfolding a statement
lapidary but also fluid, and cut
        into greatness and brevity: the un–
located but undemanding perfection of
        gigantic hinting of a world.

RAK

('*Between the aiming and the firing*
Falls the shadow'—*Pre-Columbian Proverb*.)

I

This is the House of Rak.
Where the line stops.
The end of the Family
Tree the wooden House of
Rak.

Etc.

The master and the wind writing in the
Uninhabited house: he sharpens his pen on
Uncle Jeroboam's thick, well-manicured thumb—using to
Stuff his *meerschaum* as he
Paused with a character–
Ever-so-istic gesture, down by the
Flowering *Kolkwitzia* and turned his
Tired, milk-blue, family eyes skyward and
'By the way the glass is falling' observed in a
Refined but of course trifle
Desperate

Voice.

'My aunt and all the *raznochintzy* cousins . . .' Rak
Wrote on as he . . .

—and pulling up his trouser itched his hock.

What The Clock Said:

ting (one)
ting (two)
Virtue

squealed the limpet thrush
clutching to the rain-sogged
pylon by the rose-garden

. . . and there was Uncle
In his jodhpurs and puce
Jimbaori practising his Persian the *taliq'* the

Hanging

Hand.

II

The mastiffs of Rak.
They are house-trained: devour
All day at the plaster. Consume.
It dissolves in a black breeze. They leave
The skeletons of the house: netted
Emptiness. The sun darns it.

These are
Rak his sons. They sought to evade him
And hide in the wind-forest; but
Rak dogged them.
Now they have to eat dirt but the
Master is paying.

Rak's ancestors
Are not as he writes of them they
Are buried under his thresholds, have
Fallen asleep in the ground. Nearly.
The smoke of them twines through his timbers
Clutching like a grey creeper. The nose knows it.
They assemble and cloud at the roof. But nails
Of dead men grow: they claw, tear at the beams
smoothly, like a fire. Rak's house,
The dead burn it.

III

Rak's sharping–partners
Are Dwarf, One-leg and Blind.
This is Blind's Son.

Blind's Song

The first time I loved her
I led with my Ace;
I thought that I never
Saw such a face;
I loved her in the night-time,
That night-time turned day;
But I found in the morning
She'd upped and away.

Rise and shine, sweet washing line, the wind passed by this morning.

The second time I loved her
I led my King;
But I found it wasn't
Quite the same thing:
We heard the clock ticking
All night as we lay:
Early in the morning
She upped and away,

Bells ding-dong, it won't be long, before the frosty weather.

Third time I loved her,
Led my Ten;
(Wished I'd a Full House,
To lead Ace again);
Loved her in the morning;
That morning was grey;
I watched, said nothing;
She upped, away.

Wind or rain, she'll call again, next year, sometime or never.

Last time, I
Led Two;
My last card,—
What else to do?
—She bites it like money:
'Is this pay?'
—Kitty empty.
Up, away.

Deaf and blind, sweet bars behind, and no one hears you calling.

IV

Dwarf is a Man isn't he?
Can smile. Touch things gently. Not weep.
This is his song.

Dwarf's Song

Tell me why I have to beg:—
Lacertine and theriomorph
Much excel in length of leg
Fops that condescend to Dwarf:
Fops that I'll take down a peg.

Just let Dwarfie be the norm,
Till the Beanstick People must
Empty Cloudland out, conform
Down in diesel fume and dust:
Then we'll hear the sound of storm.

Then we'll see them rage and curse
As they shuffle, as they wade
On dry land like me: rehearse
All the turns of Dwarfie's trade.
No. I have one, far worse.

That's—be lost beneath a crowd,
Boots that tower on every hand.
. . . Can't that make me Phoenix-proud?
Look, let all be grains of sand,
All are slight, are trite, are cowed.

V

One-Leg hears his song
In the keyhole all day.
The Wind is a friend.
This is wind's song.

One–Leg's Song

Sing little son.
Don't know any words.
Can't sing a tune.
But I hear your song.

Echo of noteless notes.
Black buds, they beckon all
Winter at winter sun;
All plants move underground,
Blind, where they begin
To move into spring.
Slowly the warm will come.
Soon we shall have a song.

Song of the One-Legged Man
Who has a Right Son,
That is the song to run
Sing little sun.

VI

Rak has no Woman.

Rak's Woman's Song

Because Day is so very
    You might say lit up and
Night is a time when
    You can find happy—

ness unless that is what you
    are looking for and then of
course it is very
    very very sad I like to think that

love has more in it
    or if you want less in it
than poets like to think and
    love is a poem, understand.

if I am there and you are here,
    you, dear, could call me dear;
if I could say, 'O one, two, three!'
    O how happy you would be.

VII

Rak has no song: his
Pen quivers in the floor—board like
A knife is—

This is Rak's dream:

All night he is on watch. The foe
Can float through the skeleton house like snow
Or sunlight (but black) or an ugly thought
Rak draws at, in a Rak-attack:
Shots jag a zig-zag, rat-a-tat,
Flash-crack, flash-back, crash-track.
Rak ran, his tactic.

—slow, the whiteness, the nullness

Crash goes the bric–a–brac.
'Rack Rak!' cry the house–guests, house–ghosts:
On the fired roof squats the shag–black
Battle-happy wind-bag,
Wings a-flap, wag-wag, a tic-tac,
Drums a dull rub-a-dub:

  —softness of fallen winters

Rak the last of the house; Rak's
Enemy rides the cheval-glass, track
Echoes in the rat–trap, shadow
Blackens the floor by the master he
Stands at the back of, whispering his name is
First Law of Identity:

Rak = Rak = 0.

          The Bad Dream is quick.
          In the board the nib still says

                  tick (one)
                  tick (two)

          Sleepy Clock Tock
          Slowing to

          Rak has no

          Song.

77 ✹

Rak's Song

Rain chants all day as it
   Fringes its deep labours
   Through the pot-holer's world:
Down from the dry clint

Its whiteness darkles, lace
   Swallowed in swallow-hole's
   Shafted tinkle; before all
Beginnings and after all

Endings, rain sustains the
   Rusting of rocks: felspar
   Smoothing and watering and
Hornblende softening into

Yes, rust: water's
   Touch through dark and
   The year-long lazy
Purposefulness

   Of the blindness of water
   At a man's making.

VIII

Song dust whispers as it
   Drifts. It
      Lodges. It
Becomes the pre-history of plants.

Pavane of the first green things. What
   Is a decade to them? They
      Enclose the rain.
Dew-drinkers, the ground is coloured

With a green mist. Something
   Took an upward path, is
      Alive and the seasons
Have gathered a meaning.

In a minute or millenium
The harvest is gathered. Then
(Dignity garnered in a detail)
Rising from the dead
In the face of his nephew, his son,
Unhurried, Uncle Jeroboam treads
Upstairs to his desk and
At the sunlit October window
Resumes his Persian.

The swift moons jump over the lazy dog.

A shadow, a little dust.